the hemp cookbook

ralf hiener
bettina mack
matthias schillo
stefan wirner

photography
ansgar
pudenz

ten speed press

contents

6   preface

10   hemp—a plant rediscovered

16   hemp in the kitchen

23   hemp recipes

112   basic recipes

116   the hemp idea

121   the history of hemp

122   the revolution in the kitchen

124   the people

132   epilogue

136   glossary

138   legal status

140   hemp resources

142   recipes from a to z

preface

Hemp is currently undergoing a renaissance. Many states are moving toward making the cultivation and sale of THC-free varieties legal once again. Though in its infancy, a new hemp industry is slowly developing in the Americas. Processing capacity needs to be expanded and a distribution system organized. Insulation, wall coatings, and floor coverings, as well as clothing, made of hemp are already being produced.

The entire product chain, from cultivation through processing to consumption, can be completed locally–on local farmland, in small- to medium-sized businesses, and without requiring significant investment in transportation. The ecological advantages are obvious, and this is true of all products, including, of course, hemp as a food product. Because hemp seeds contain many essential unsaturated fatty acids, dishes prepared with hemp are also healthful.

Although spaghetti al dente with plenty of garlic remains an all-time favorite, some of the hemp dishes here will quickly grow on you. A hemp cookbook then, becomes essential, especially one that, in addition to many other dishes, includes a recipe for Raisin Noodles in Hemp-honey Sauce. Hemp and Vegetable Ravioli on Red Lentils and Pork Rib Roast in Hemp-beer Sauce will also surprise and delight. With this hemp cookbook, an idea is suddenly transformed into something palpable that we can all experience–food. Anyone who is interested can experiment and find out for themselves why hemp represents such a tremendous enrichment to our diet.

Bon appetit!

M. Prats

hemp
a plant is rediscovered

The history of hemp reads like a detective novel. Its many uses have been known for centuries—and hemp could become a good friend in our daily lives.

Hemp—as a food product, as a building material, as a fuel, or as a medicine—was rediscovered just a few years ago. This rediscovery was triggered by a book written by Jack Herer, *The Emperor Wears No Clothes: Hemp and the Marijuana Conspiracy.* Herer presented for the first time the history of the hemp prohibition and the people behind it, as well as the history and the possibilities offered by hemp as a viable crop. A worldwide hemp movement has arisen since then. The fact that hemp is not just a narcotic but also a food and a raw material has been common knowledge for some time now.

Now hemp seeds as well as clothing, paper, building materials, paints, detergents, and cooking oils—all made of imported hemp—are available (see "Hemp Resources," p. 140). And if states begin to allow commercial hemp development, *non*imported hemp will soon be available.

Years ago, encouraged by Herer's book, we began developing dishes made with hemp in the kitchen of our restaurant, Zum Weissen Hirsch (The

White Buck). For us, our guests' considerable enthusiasm for hemp dishes served as both an affirmation and an incentive. To offer these dishes to a larger group of people, we decided to write the hemp cookbook that you, dear readers, now hold in your hands.

Not just delicious, but also extremely healthful! As a food product, hemp still offers quite a few surprises.

Hemp was an important part of our cuisine for centuries. Once it was banned from our cuisine for no good reason, we had to prove that hemp is not only extremely easy to digest, but that it is also flavorful. Its high fatty- and amino-acid content makes it very nutritious and healthful. Although hemp ought to be a good old friend it is, in fact, a newcomer in today's kitchen. We have only gradually begun to understand the variety hemp offers as a food product. Hemp, in the form of seeds, oil, flour, or meal, can be used everywhere, from appetizers through main courses to desserts. The recipes presented here represent only a small selection and are meant to provide the initial incentive to those who want to become more familiar with hemp in the kitchen. We deliberately view ourselves as part of the new hemp movement, because we believe that hemp embodies an environmentally friendly alternative in many areas of life. If we can relearn what we have almost forgotten, hemp can become the renewable resource of the next century. For many years, the hemp prohibition stood in the way of a promising path toward an economy that functions while consuming fewer raw materials. It also failed to achieve its objective of persuading millions of marijuana smokers worldwide to give up their traditional drug. The hemp to which we refer in this book as a food product consists of those low-THC varieties that are commercially available today and that produce no narcotic effects when consumed. For us, hemp has long been a cooking ingredient we don't want to do without. We hope that this hemp cookbook expresses the enjoyment and enthusiasm we experience when we cook with hemp, and hope that you, too, enjoy your new encounter with hemp. Here's to hemp making its way back to everyone's plate before long.

Hemp—just cook it!

Hemp is a sensible alternative, both economically and ecologically. A robust plant, hemp grows back rapidly after cultivation without the need for chemical fertilizers.

hemp in the kitchen

For centuries hemp, as a basic food, was a fundamental part of the diet among many peoples of the world. As one of mankind's oldest useful plants, it is part of our cultural heritage. While archaeologists and historians date its first use to about 10,000 B.C., hemp was indigenous in all cultures of the Middle East, Asia Minor, India, Japan, Europe, and Africa by no later than 2700 B.C. Since then, it has been used as a raw material, as medicine, and as food. Because of hemp's outstanding nutritional value, it became *the* plant in times of famine. For example, the people of Australia survived two lengthy famines during the 1800s by consuming hemp seeds and leaves. In many other countries, hemp was a perfectly normal and conventional food, and no one would ever have thought of banning it because of its additional narcotic properties, properties that are only found in certain hemp varieties.

For us, however, hemp as an ingredient in a wide variety of dishes was a discovery of taste. Its nutty overtones refine many meat and fish dishes and

give them a very special aroma. However, hemp should be used sparingly in certain dishes so that its taste does not overpower everything else. Although cooking with hemp is sometimes a little more involved, hemp pancakes, gratins with a hemp crust, or salads with hemp seeds sprinkled on top stand a good chance of finding their way back to our conventional daily menu.

First we must reacquaint ourselves with hemp as a food product. Find a good health food store that sells hemp products and be sure to check out "Hemp Resources" at the back of this book for places where you can order hemp food products.

Before you try one of the dishes presented in this cookbook, you can start out by making a simple and delicious snack of hemp seeds:

hemp
17

Hemp Snack To make this snack, first wash the hemp seeds. Place the seeds in a container filled with water so that heavier unwanted components, such as sand or small pebbles, will sink to the bottom. Use a strainer to skim off the seeds floating on the surface. Drain any remaining water from the seeds. Without using any oil, roast them in a pan for 2 to 3 minutes over a low flame. Now the seeds will release their special aroma. Remove them from the stove before they begin to pop and turn darker. Sprinkle on a little salt and your hemp snack is ready to enjoy. The roasted hemp seeds are both a delicious snack and a wonderful ingredient for garnishing salads, sauces, and many main courses (but be careful while chewing, as the shells of the hemp seeds easily become stuck between your teeth).

Hemp Meal Hemp meal is produced by crushing the roasted hemp seeds with a mortar and pestle. It can be used in the same way as wheat meal or oatmeal, such as in muesli or hot cereal, or as an ingredient in many other dishes, as our recipes will demonstrate.

Hemp Flour Hemp flour is made by pulverizing the hemp seeds. Although it is characterized by excellent nutritional value, hemp flour is difficult to use on its own because it tends to crumble.*

*To stop pastry from crumbling, the flour used must have good agglutination properties–try adding other types of flour.

Hemp Oil

Hemp oil is obtained by pressing the seeds. Because of its delicate manufacturing process, this oil only keeps for a short time. Once a bottle has been opened, it should be stored in a cool, dark place and used up quickly. Hemp oil becomes rancid and loses its nutritional properties as soon as it comes into contact with air and light. Furthermore, it should not be used for frying and sautéing, because heat destroys the oil's valuable components and can even make it indigestible. Hemp oil shares these problems with other high-quality oils that contain essential fatty acids—oils that are so healthful precisely because, like hemp oil, they are not refined and treated. However, recent developments in processing suggest that hemp oil with a longer shelf life will soon become available on the market.

Hemp Salad

The leaves of the hemp plant can also be used in salads. However, as fresh hemp leaves are currently unavailable in stores, we have not included recipes for them in this

The hemp seed contains all essential amino acids, as well as the essential fatty acids that are important for a well-functioning immune system.

cookbook. Hemp's contribution to a healthful diet, a factor which should not be underestimated, will help pave the way for hemp's return to the kitchen. As a wide variety of scientific studies have demonstrated, no other plant can match hemp for its nutritional value. For example, the American nutritionist Udo Erasmus concludes the following: "Because of its unusually well-balanced fatty acid profile, you could consume hemp oil for the rest of your life without suffering a deficiency in essential fatty acids. Its gamma-linolenic acid (GLA) content makes hemp oil unique among the edible oils." Other scientists, such as William Eidlemann and R. Lee Hamilton of the University of California, credit hemp as a potential quick fix to the world's nutrition problems. Even if one does not share this optimistic viewpoint, scientists have certainly reached a consensus that a diet that includes hemp in its various forms—as oil, meal, or seeds—is considered healthful and easy to digest. As a therapeutic agent, hemp is supposedly effective in treating many diet-related disorders ranging from immune diseases, cardiovascular diseases, and metabolic disorders to neuroderma-titis. The inclusion of hemp in one's diet may improve the appearance of skin, hair, and eyes; clean the arteries; and reinforce cerebral functions. Hemp certainly deserves its chance for a new beginning as a normal, conventional food product and as a component of our diet. If demand for hemp as a food product increases in the future, cultivation will be simplified and new processes to extend the shelf life of the oil will become readily available; then nothing will stand in the way of hemp making its comeback into the kitchen.

In addition to the terms described above, the "Glossary" at the end of this book explains various terms concerning hemp, while the "Hemp Resources" section (page 140) provides a list of literature about hemp.

recipe yields

Unless otherwise noted, the ingredients used in the recipes are calculated for four people. Basic recipes, such as those for vegetable or Meat Stock, are provided after this recipe section, beginning on page 112.

note: We have not given amounts for the use of fresh herbs in recipes throughout the book. These amounts depend on taste, but a general rule is to use 1–2 teaspoons per portion of all herbs combined.

appetizers

fresh salads,

fine soups,

and other

hors d'oeuvres

carpaccio of beef
with hemp oil and romano

ingredients

Fresh herbs (such as
  tarragon, chervil, parsley,
  lemon thyme, chives,
  cilantro), chopped
3 tablespoons hemp meal
Salt
Freshly ground pepper
10 ounces beef fillet
Juice from ½ lime
5 tablespoons hemp oil
4 ounces Romano cheese

note: Beef must be prepared ahead of time
and frozen for at least 12 hours.

1 Crush herbs, hemp meal, salt, and pepper in a
mortar and work into a paste.

2 Remove fat and tendons from the meat and rub
the paste onto the fillet. Wrap the fillet in plastic
wrap and keep in the freezer for at least 12 hours.

3 Remove the fillet from the freezer (no need to
thaw), remove the wrap, and use a slicing
machine to cut the fillet into paper-thin slices.

4 Immediately arrange the slices on plates and
sprinkle with lime juice and hemp oil. Grate
Romano or another Italian hard cheese onto the
slices and serve immediately.

tip: Try modifying the taste by using sage
instead of coriander.

lamb's lettuce
with hemp-potato vinaigrette

1 Wash the lamb's lettuce several times (lamb's lettuce is often very sandy).

2 Drain in a colander.

3 Mash the boiled potatoes for the vinaigrette. Boil the stock with the onion, pour over the potatoes, and stir.

4 Add the vinegar, hemp oil, hemp meal, salt, and pepper and mix well.

5 Place the lamb's lettuce onto plates and pour vinaigrette over it.

tip: Serve with crispy fried strips of bacon and croutons—a delicious snack!

ingredients

1 pound lamb's lettuce (also
  sold as mâche)

vinaigrette
$\frac{1}{4}$ pound boiled potatoes
$\frac{1}{3}$ cup Vegetable Stock
  (page 113)
1 tablespoon finely
  chopped onion
$\frac{1}{4}$ cup white wine vinegar
$\frac{1}{4}$ cup hemp oil
4 tablespoons hemp meal
Salt
Pepper

hemp
29

mixed greens
with hemp oil and hemp seeds

ingredients

Available greens (such as
red leaf, white leaf, oak
leaf lettuce; curly endive;
escarole)

vinaigrette*
¼ cup vegetable oil
¼ cup hemp oil
3 tablespoons sherry
vinegar
1 teaspoon finely diced
onion
½ teaspoon mustard
Salt and pepper to taste
Fresh herbs (optional)
Carrots (optional)
Nasturtium flowers
(optional)
Sprouts (optional)
4 tablespoons freshly
roasted hemp seeds

*This amount is enough for
2 salads (keep the remaining
vinaigrette refrigerated in a jar).

1 Clean and wash the greens. Allow to drip dry
in a colander or dry in a salad spinner.

2 To make the vinaigrette, thoroughly mix all
ingredients in a food processor or blender
until you obtain a creamy sauce. (Balsamic vinegar
can be used instead of the sherry vinegar–or,
when added to sherry vinegar, the smoother
taste of a good balsamic vinegar tones down the
sharpness.)

3 Toss the greens with the dressing and place
onto a plate. Garnish with herbs, carrots,
nasturtiums, and sprouts.

4 Sprinkle the hemp seeds over the salad.

tip: Chicory loses its bitter taste when it is soaked in lukewarm water for about 10 minutes.

cucumber soup
with hemp dumplings

1 Peel, core, and dice the cucumbers.

2 Sauté in butter with onion until translucent, add the white wine and stock. Simmer for about 15 minutes.

3 To make the dumplings, combine all ingredients and stir into a smooth dough.

4 Using a spoon, shape small dumplings and slide them into boiling salted water.

5 As soon as the dumplings float to the top, they are ready and can be carefully removed from the boiling water.

6 Pureé the soup. Add salt, pepper, and lemon juice to taste, and flavor with dill.

7 Serve the soup with the hemp dumplings in deep dishes.

ingredients

soup
2 cucumbers
3 tablespoons butter
2 tablespoons finely diced
 onion
$^1/_3$ cup white wine
2 cups Meat Stock
 (page 113)
Lemon juice
Salt
Pepper
1 bunch dill, finely chopped

dumplings
$^1/_2$ cup flour
1 tablespoon hemp meal
2 tablespoons water
1 egg
Salt
Pepper
Nutmeg

hemp
33

hemp-pancake soup

pancakes
¾ cup milk
3 eggs
2 tablespoons hemp meal
½ cup flour
Salt
Nutmeg
3 tablespoons butter

4 cups Meat Stock
  (page 113)

Chives, finely chopped

1 Stir together milk, eggs, hemp meal, flour, salt, and nutmeg. Allow to rise for half an hour, then fry small hemp pancakes in butter. Cut these pancakes into narrow strips.

2 Arrange the hemp-pancake strips in deep bowls and fill the bowls with the hot Meat Stock. Sprinkle with chives and serve.

tip: This soup marks the beginning of a typical menu from Germany's Baden region. The beef brisket that was cooked to make the Meat Stock can be served with horseradish sauce and boiled potatoes as a main course.

hemp-vegetable soup

1 Finely dice the vegetables and onion, sauté lightly in butter; add salt and white wine, and Meat Stock. Simmer for about 15 minutes.

2 Using a strainer, remove half of the vegetables and set aside.

3 Pureé the soup and bring to a boil again. Add cream and the vegetables that were removed earlier. Season to taste.

4 Sprinkle roasted hemp seeds and herbs into the soup. Drizzle a little hemp oil on the soup and serve hot.

variation: Sprinkle a little curry powder onto the vegetables while they are being sautéed.

ingredients

2 carrots
1 leek
1 stalk of celery
1 onion
3 tablespoons butter
Salt
4 tablespoons white wine
2½ cups Meat Stock
  (page 113)
4 tablespoons cream
4 tablespoons roasted
  hemp seeds
Fresh herbs (such as
  parsley, chervil, or chives),
  finely chopped
Hemp oil

hemp
37

hemp quiche

ingredients

dough
⅓ cup hemp flour
1½ cups wheat flour
¼ cup water
7 tablespoons butter
Pinch of salt

filling
⅓ cup mushrooms (white, oyster, or porcini, depending on the season), chopped
1 tablespoon finely diced onion
1 leek, cut into strips
½ cup cream
2 eggs
Salt
Pepper

1½ ounces grated Gruyère cheese
2 tablespoons roasted hemp seeds

1 Preheat oven to 350°.

2 To make the dough, place the ingredients in a bowl and knead until smooth. Set aside in a cool place for ½ hour.

3 To make the filling, sauté the mushrooms, onion, and leeks in butter and season to taste. Set aside to cool.

4 In a separate bowl, beat the cream and eggs, then season with salt and pepper. Add cooled vegetables.

5 Roll out the dough to a thickness of ¼ inch and place into a medium-sized, buttered quiche or pie pan. Pull up the edges of the dough slightly.

6 Pour the filling onto the dough. Sprinkle grated cheese and hemp seeds on top and bake for about 25 minutes or until top is golden brown. Cut the quiche into pieces and serve with a fresh green salad.

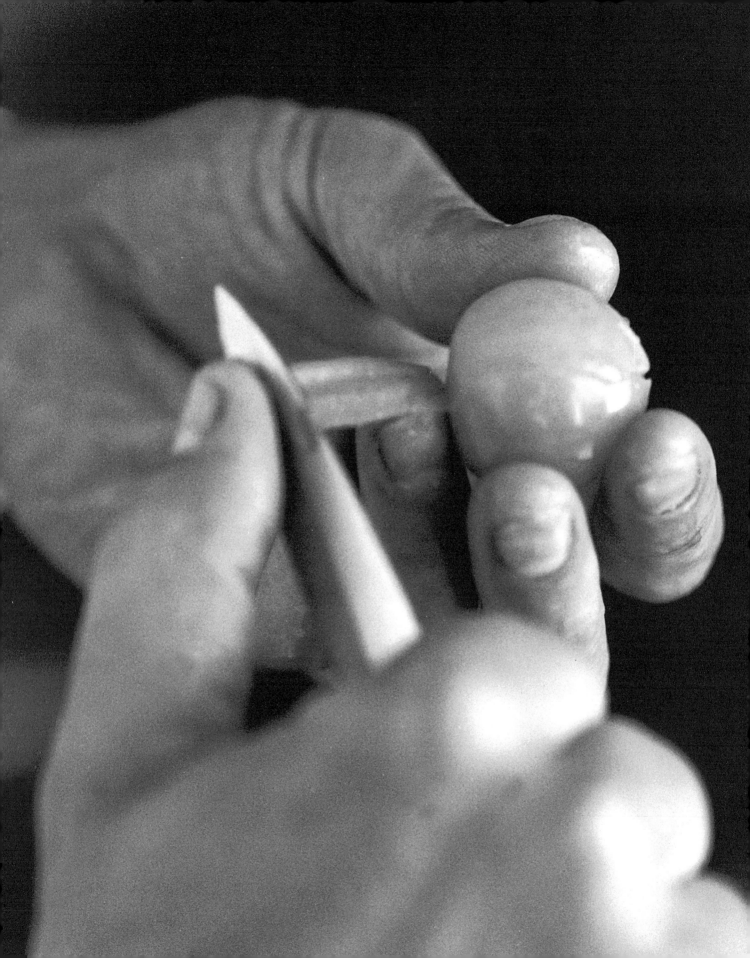

hemp-tomato crostini

1 Cut the baguette into 1-inch-thick slices.

2 Pour boiling water over the tomatoes, then peel, quarter, and core. Cut the flesh of the tomatoes into small cubes.

3 Preheat broiler.

4 Sauté the shallots and garlic in olive oil. Add olives and tomatoes and sauté briefly.

5 Season with salt and pepper, add roasted hemp seeds, and season to taste with fresh herbs.

6 Spread olive oil onto the baguette slices and toast on both sides until golden. Top with the sautéed tomatoes, sprinkle with grated cheese, and broil until crispy.

tip: You can create a particularly delicious version of this dish by using goat cheese for the crisp topping.

ingredients

1 baguette or ciabatta loaf

8 tomatoes

4 tablespoons finely diced shallots

1 tablespoon finely chopped garlic

2 tablespoons olive oil

12 black olives, pitted

Salt

Pepper

4 tablespoons roasted hemp seeds

Fresh herbs (basil, thyme, rosemary), as available

3 1/2 ounces grated Parmesan cheese

hemp
41

potato salad
with hemp-oil vinaigrette

ingredients

1 pound potatoes

½ cup Meat Stock
(page 113)

4 tablespoons finely diced
onion

3½ tablespoons white wine
vinegar

Salt

Pepper

½ teaspoon nutmeg

1 bunch chives, minced

5½ tablespoons hemp oil

4 tablespoons freshly
roasted hemp seeds

1 Boil, peel, and thinly slice the potatoes while still warm. Boil the stock with the onion and vinegar; pour over the potato slices. Soak for about 30 minutes.

2 Season with salt, pepper, nutmeg, and chives to taste. Add the oil, and sprinkle with hemp seeds.

tip: Try adding a few finely diced gherkins to the potato salad.

note: Don't worry if the potatoes are slightly mushy—that's the correct consistency for this recipe.

vegetarian

tasty, meatless

main courses

hemp patties

ingredients

1/3 pound finely diced
  vegetables (carrots, leeks,
  kohlrabi, spring onions)
2 tablespoons finely diced
  onion
2 tablespoons butter
2 cups millet flakes
2 cups Vegetable Stock
(page 113)
Salt
Pepper
2 eggs
1/2 cup hemp meal
Fresh herbs (parsley,
  chervil, tarragon) to taste,
  finely chopped
3 tablespoons clarified
  butter

1 Sauté the vegetables and onion in butter, add
the millet flakes and the stock. Season with salt
and pepper to taste.

2 Simmer for 2 to 3 minutes and then remove
from the stove. Allow to cool a little, then fold in
the eggs.

3 Add the hemp meal and herbs. The mixture
should not be so wet that it will stick to your
hands while it is being shaped into patties. Cool
the mixture well and then shape into patties.
Sauté the patties in clarified butter over moderate heat until golden brown.

tip: These patties can be made using all kinds
of vegetables. They also taste good on rolls as
"hemp burgers."

hemp and vegetable ravioli
on red lentils

1 To make the dough, thoroughly knead the ingredients and set aside for 1 hour.

2 To make the filling, chop the vegetables into small cubes, sauté in butter, and cook over low heat until tender. Season with salt, pepper, and herbs.

3 Place the dough onto a floured surface and, using a rolling pin, roll to a very thin consistency. Place evenly spaced portions of the filling onto half of the dough, allowing enough room so that the ravioli can later be cut out.

4 Brush egg white onto the spaces between the filling. Fold the upper half of the dough over the lower half, and press the spaces between portions into place. Using a pasta wheel, cut out individual ravioli and drop them into boiling salted water. Boil for about 5 minutes. The ravioli are done when they float to the top.

5 To make the red lentils, sauté the onion in butter until translucent. Add the lentils and sauté briefly. Add the vinegar and the stock. Boil for 7 to 8 minutes, stirring frequently. Toward the end of the cooking time, add cream and herbs.

6 Place some lentils on the center of each plate and surround with ravioli.

a hearty variation: Sauté finely chopped cubes of bacon with the lentils.

ingredients

dough
2 cups flour
5 tablespoons hemp meal
⅔ cup semolina
3 eggs
2 egg yolks
¼ teaspoon salt

filling
3 carrots
1 celery root
1 leek (or a different vegetable, if desired)
2 tablespoons butter
Salt
Pepper
Fresh herbs (parsley, chervil, tarragon) to taste, finely chopped

lentils
2 tablespoons finely diced onion
2 tablespoons butter
2 cups red lentils
3 tablespoons balsamic vinegar
1 cup Vegetable Stock (page 113)
½ cup cream
Fresh herbs

hemp
49

hemp gnocchi
with curried carrots

ingredients

gnocchi dough

1 pound ricotta cheese
¹/₃ cup hemp meal
1 cup flour
1 egg
1 egg yolk
Clarified butter
Fresh sage leaves, finely
  chopped

curried carrots

1 pound carrots
2 tablespoons finely diced
  onion
4 tablespoons butter
1 tablespoon curry powder
¹/₂ cup Vegetable Stock
  (page 113)

1 To make the dough, squeeze any excess water out of the ricotta cheese. Combine the cheese with hemp meal, flour, egg, and egg yolk, and work into a smooth dough. Refrigerate for 1 hour.

2 To make the curried carrots, peel and slice the carrots. In a pot, sauté the onion in butter until translucent, then dust with curry powder. Add the sliced carrots and Vegetable Stock. Cook until carrots are tender, and keep warm.

3 On a floured surface, shape the dough into a roll and cut it into 1-inch-thick pieces.

4 Boil the gnocchi in salted water until they rise to the surface. Drain the gnocchi well in a colander (otherwise they will stick to the pan during frying) and fry in clarified butter until golden brown. Shortly before removing from the pan, add the sage.

5 Serve with the curried carrots.

hemp-semolina slices
with chanterelle mushrooms

1 To make the dough, boil the milk, stock, butter, and hemp meal, then add salt and stir in the semolina. Stir constantly over low heat until the mixture separates from the pot. Remove from the stove and allow to cool. Gradually fold in the egg yolks.

2 Spread a ¾-inch layer of the semolina mixture onto a buttered baking sheet and refrigerate.

3 Preheat broiler.

4 Sauté the mushrooms and onion in clarified butter, and season to taste with salt, pepper, garlic, and herbs.

5 Using a cookie cutter, punch out half-moon pieces of the cooled semolina mixture, sprinkle with grated cheese, and broil for about 10 minutes, or until golden brown.

6 Arrange the semolina slices on a plate in a star-shaped pattern, add the mushrooms, and serve.

ingredients

semolina dough
1 quart whole milk
1 cup Vegetable Stock
(page 113)
4 tablespoons butter
2 tablespoons hemp meal
Salt
1 cup semolina
2 egg yolks

mushroom mixture
$\frac{2}{3}$ pound porcini
  mushrooms, washed,
  trimmed, and sliced
$\frac{1}{2}$ pound chanterelle
  mushrooms
2 tablespoons finely diced
  onion
3 tablespoons clarified
  butter
Salt
Pepper
1 clove garlic
Fresh herbs (parsley,
  chives, chervil) to taste,
  finely chopped

hemp
53

hemp and potato gratin

ingredients

1 clove garlic

2 teaspoons butter

1¾ pounds potatoes

2 cups milk

1 cup heavy cream

Salt

Pepper

Nutmeg

4 tablespoons hemp meal

Grated Swiss cheese
  (optional)

1 Preheat oven to 350°.

2 Rub a baking dish with garlic and butter. Cut potatoes into very thin slices using a knife or a vegetable slicer and arrange in the baking dish.

3 Bring milk and cream to a boil. Add salt, pepper, and nutmeg to taste. Pour over the potatoes while hot and sprinkle hemp meal on top.

4 Bake for 30 minutes, then reduce the heat to 325° and bake for about 20 minutes more. Sprinkle grated cheese over the gratin to give it a hearty flavor.

tip: Hemp and potato gratin can be served as a meal in itself or as an accompaniment to a fish entrée. If you choose to serve the gratin as a side dish, just divide the above amounts in half.

hemp and potato dumplings
with tomato-leek garnish

ingredients

dumplings
1 ¼ pounds potatoes, boiled
  in their skins and cooked
  a day in advance
⅔ cup flour
4 ounces ricotta cheese
2 eggs
Nutmeg
3 tablespoons hemp meal
Clarified butter

garnish
8 tomatoes
1 leek
2 tablespoons butter
2 tablespoons finely
  diced onion
Salt
Pepper
¼ cup cream
1 bunch chives, minced

note: The potatoes should be cooked a day ahead of time.

1 Peel the potatoes and force through a sieve. Mix in flour, cheese, and eggs. Add salt, pepper, and nutmeg to taste. Add hemp meal and quickly work into a dough.

2 Form small dumplings. Fry in clarified butter over moderate heat until golden brown, and keep in a warm place.

3 To make the garnish, pour hot water over the tomatoes or briefly immerse them in boiling water.

4 Remove tomato skins. Quarter and core the tomatoes and cut the flesh into cubes.

5 Slice the leek lengthwise, wash well, and cut into strips. Sauté in butter with the onion, then season with salt and pepper to taste. Add the tomatoes and simmer for about 2 minutes.

6 Add the cream and chives. Arrange the tomato mixture in the center of each plate, surround with dumplings, and serve.

hemp and cabbage strudel

ingredients

dough
2 cups flour
2 tablespoons hemp meal
½ cup lukewarm water
1 tablespoon hemp oil

filling
1 head of white cabbage
   (about 2 pounds), thinly
   sliced
2 tablespoons finely diced
   onion
2 tablespoons butter
½ cup Vegetable Stock
   (page 113)
Salt
Pepper
Caraway seeds (optional)
Melted butter to brush
   onto the strudel
3 tablespoons sesame
   seeds
3 tablespoons roasted
   hemp seeds
Hemp-butter Sauce
   (page 81)

1 Knead the flour, hemp meal, water, and hemp oil into a strudel dough. Wrap in foil and allow to sit for 1 hour.

2 To make the filling, sauté the cabbage and onion in butter. Add the stock, season with salt, pepper, and caraway seeds to taste. Simmer until tender (about 20 minutes). Set aside in a cool place.

3 Preheat oven to 375°.

4 Roll out the strudel dough with a pasta roller, then draw out the dough with your hands from center to edges until it is very thin (almost transparent). Spread onto a cloth. The dough should be so thin that one could almost read a newspaper through it.

5 Distribute the cooled cabbage filling onto the dough and roll it up, using a damp cloth. Brush with melted butter and sprinkle sesame seeds and hemp seeds on top. Place onto a buttered baking sheet and bake for 25 to 30 minutes. Brush melted butter onto the strudel several times while it is baking. Allow to sit for 10 minutes after baking.

6 Cut the strudel into uniform pieces and serve with Hemp-butter Sauce.

hemp crepes
with mushrooms

1 To make the dough, combine milk, flour, hemp meal, eggs and egg yolk, and work into a smooth batter. Let the batter stand for ½ hour.

2 Sauté the mushrooms and vegetables in the clarified butter.

3 Cool the vegetable-mushroom filling and then season to taste with salt, pepper, nutmeg, and herbs.

4 Preheat broiler.

5 Melt the clarified butter in a frying pan. Ladle batter into pan to form small crepes. Then spoon the filling onto the crepes and roll them up. Arrange on ovenproof plates, sprinkle grated cheese on top, and broil for 10 minutes.

tip: The filling described here is intended merely as a suggestion. Feel free to let your imagination run wild!

ingredients

batter
1¼ cups milk
1 cup flour
3 tablespoons hemp meal
3 eggs
1 egg yolk
4 tablespoons butter for
  frying

filling
1⅓ pound mushrooms
  (champignons, oyster,
  shiitakes, chanterelles),
  sliced
1 cup julienned vegetables
  (carrots, rutabagas, leeks,
  bell peppers)
3 tablespoons clarified
  butter
Salt
Pepper
Nutmeg
Fresh herbs to taste

4 ounces grated Gruyère
  cheese

hemp
61

hemp and saffron risotto
with chanterelles

ingredients

1 pound chanterelles
5 tablespoons butter
1⅓ pounds risotto rice
⅓ cup finely diced onion
Salt
1 cup white wine
8 cups Vegetable Stock
   (page 113)
A few saffron threads
⅓ cup finely diced
   vegetables (carrots, leek,
   celery)
4 tablespoons roasted
   hemp seeds
4 ounces grated Parmesan
   cheese

1 Thoroughly clean the chanterelles. Shake them dry in a salad spinner or a colander to prevent them from soaking up water. Set aside.

2 In a tall pot, briefly sauté the rice and onion in half of the butter. Season with salt and add white wine and some of the stock. Simmer, stirring frequently.

3 Gradually add the remaining stock while stirring constantly so that the rice can absorb the liquid as effectively as possible.

4 Shortly before the end of the cooking period (about 15 minutes), add the saffron and vegetables and continue to cook.

5 Remove the pot from the heat and stir in the hemp seeds, butter, and grated cheese.

6 Briefly sauté the chanterelles in the remaining butter and arrange on a plate with the risotto.

hemp and sage polenta
with pan-roasted bell peppers

1 Add salt and half of the olive oil to the water and bring to a boil.

2 Toss in the sage and roasted hemp seeds. Reduce the heat.

3 Slowly add the polenta while stirring constantly. Continue to stir, allowing the steam to escape, until the water is absorbed and the polenta is firm.

4 Spread the mixture onto a damp board (to a thickness of 1/3 to 1/2 inch) and allow it to cool. Cut diagonally in a crisscross pattern. Using the remaining olive oil, brown the polenta slices on both sides in a frying pan.

5 Clean the bell peppers and cut into small pieces. Sauté with garlic in olive oil and season with salt and pepper to taste.

6 Spread the mixture onto the polenta slices and serve immediately.

ingredients

polenta slices
Pinch of salt
2 tablespoons olive oil
1 quart water
1 bunch fresh sage, finely chopped
3 tablespoons roasted hemp seeds
1 1/2 cups polenta (cornmeal)

2 bell peppers
1 clove garlic, chopped
Olive oil
Salt
White pepper

hemp
65

hemp spätzle
with tomatoes and goat cheese

ingredients

spätzle

3½ cups flour
1 cup hemp meal
9 eggs
2 egg yolks
Salt
1 teaspoon nutmeg
2 tablespoons butter

4 tomatoes, sliced
7 ounces goat cheese, diced

1 In a large bowl, mix flour, hemp meal, eggs, egg yolks, salt, and nutmeg and knead into a light dough, with your hands.

2 Place the dough onto a wooden board. Using a knife, scrape thin strips into boiling salted water.

3 Preheat broiler.

4 Slow boil the spätzle until they float to the top of the pot. Remove with a strainer and rinse in cold water.

5 Dry in a colander, then toss with butter in a pan over medium heat and salt to taste.

6 Arrange the spätzle in the middle of plates, surround with the tomatoes and goat cheese, and broil for about 5 minutes.

a hearty variation: Serve the spätzle with onion slices roasted with garlic and thyme. Or serve the hemp spätzle as a side dish, without the tomatoes and goat cheese (use half the above amounts).

potato dumplings
with a hemp filling

note: The potatoes should be cooked a day ahead of time.

1 To make the dumplings, peel the potatoes, then press them through a sieve. Combine with the remaining dumpling ingredients and set aside in a cool place.

2 To make the filling, pass the cheese through a sieve. Fold in the hemp meal and hemp oil. Season to taste with salt, pepper, nutmeg, and thyme.

3 Divide the potato dough into 12 even pieces and flatten. Place some filling in the middle of each piece and shape into dumplings. Simmer the dumplings in salted water until they rise to the surface.

4 Depending on your preference, serve the dumplings with fresh, sautéed mushrooms or vegetable ragout.

ingredients

dumplings
5 peeled potatoes, boiled in their skins and cooked a day in advance
1 cup flour
3½ tablespoons butter
3 eggs
Salt

filling
7 ounces feta cheese
3 tablespoons hemp meal
1 teaspoon hemp oil
Salt
Pepper
½ teaspoon nutmeg
Fresh thyme

hemp
69

spaghetti
with hemp and almond pesto

ingredients

1½ pounds semolina
  spaghetti
Salt

pesto
⅓ cup roasted hemp seeds
⅓ cup sliced almonds
1 bunch fresh basil
2 tablespoons hemp oil
2 tablespoons olive oil
3 ounces grated Parmesan
  cheese

1 Boil the spaghetti in rapidly boiling salted water until al dente. Drain and rinse.

2 To make the pesto, place the hemp seeds, almonds, basil, hemp oil, and olive oil in a mortar. Grind into a paste, folding in almost all the cheese at the end.

3 Heat the spaghetti in a pan with olive oil and butter and salt to taste. Heat (but do not boil) the pesto in a pot.

4 Spoon pesto on top of spaghetti, and serve with grated Parmesan cheese.

tip: Finely chopped tomatoes added to the pesto will give the dish an attractive color and a refreshing taste.

fish + meat

sophisticated

coastal and

country dishes

bouillabaisse

of freshwater fish with hemp and semolina dumplings

ingredients

About 2½ pounds fresh-
  water fish (trout, pike,
  perch, pike perch, salmon,
  char), as available
5 medium potatoes, peeled
  and quartered
2 carrots
1 zucchini
½ leek
4 tomatoes, skinned and
  diced
Fresh herbs (dill, parsley,
  chives), finely chopped

dumplings

7 tablespoons softened
  butter, whipped until
  foamy
3 eggs
2 tablespoons hemp meal
½ teaspoon nutmeg
3½ ounces semolina

1 Fillet the fish (or have it filleted where you pur-
chase it). Prepare a Fish Stock with the bones
and discarded portions of the fish (see page 112).

2 To make the dumplings, stir the butter, eggs,
hemp meal, nutmeg, and semolina into a supple
mixture and set aside for ½ hour.

3 Using two small teaspoons, shape the dough
into small dumplings and boil in salted water for
about 10 minutes. Set aside the pot containing
the dumplings.

4 In the Fish Stock, cook the potatoes and vegetables until tender. Remove them and set aside.

5 Poach the fish fillets in the Fish Stock for 5
minutes.

6 Place the fillets, potatoes, and vegetables into
deep bowls.

7 Drain the dumplings. Add them to the deep
bowls and pour the Fish Stock on top. Sprinkle
with herbs to taste and serve.

serves six

a delicious variation: Add a few threads of
saffron to the stock just before serving.

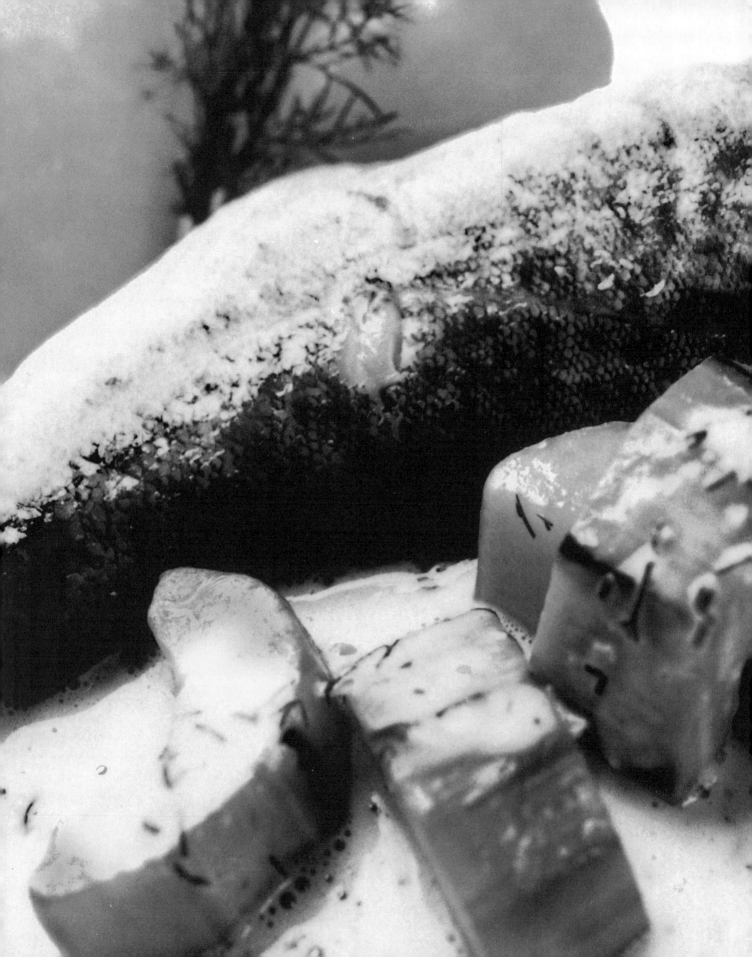

hemp-steamed cod
with dill sauce

1 Dress and clean the fish. Carefully remove all traces of blood. Cut off the head.

2 Thoroughly rinse inside and outside of fish with cold water.

3 Prepare a Fish Stock with the bones (see page 112). Add the hemp meal and wine to the stock.

4 Salt the fish on both sides, drizzle with lemon juice, and place with vegetables into a steamer insert.

5 Place the steamer insert into a pot and cover with a lid. Steam for 10 to 12 minutes.

6 To prepare the dill sauce, simmer the shallot in the white wine.

7 Remove from the heat and stir in the chilled butter, producing a creamy sauce.

8 Season to taste with salt, pepper, lemon juice, and dill.

9 Remove the fish from the steamer, cut into pieces, and arrange on plates with the sauce. Serve with boiled potatoes or rice.

note: The careful mode of preparation outlined in steps 1 and 2 works with any kind of fish. It is particularly well suited for cod, as it falls apart easily.

ingredients

4 young cod, about
  3 pounds total
2 cups water
½ cup Fish Stock (page 112)
5 tablespoons hemp meal
1 cup white wine
Salt
Lemon juice
1 bunch of vegetables
  (1 medium carrot, ½ leek,
  1 celery stalk, ½ onion),
  chopped

sauce
1 teaspoon finely chopped
  shallot
1½ cups dry white wine
2 sticks butter, chilled
Lemon juice
4 tablespoons fresh dill,
  chopped

hemp
77

fillet of pike
with hemp-horseradish crust

ingredients

6 tablespoons softened
  butter
⅓ cup bread crumbs
3 tablespoons fresh horse-
  radish, very finely grated
2 tablespoons hemp meal
Salt
Pepper
4 pike fillets, ⅓ pound each
Flour to coat fish
Clarified butter
Lemon juice

1 To prepare the hemp-horseradish crust, whip the butter with a wire whisk until creamy.

2 Preheat broiler.

3 Add the bread crumbs, horseradish, and hemp meal to the butter. Season with salt and pepper to taste and mix thoroughly. Set aside in a cool place.

4 Salt the pike fillets, dip in flour, and fry in clarified butter on both sides, over medium heat, for 5 to 6 minutes. Drizzle with lemon juice.

5 Brush the hemp-horseradish mixture onto the pike fillets and cook under the broiler for 1 or 2 minutes, until golden.

6 Serve with fried potatoes. Red beet salad is also a wonderful complement to this dish.

pike perch fillet
with hemp-butter sauce

1 Salt and pepper the pike perch fillets and roll in flour. Fry on both sides in clarified butter for 4 to 5 minutes over moderate heat. Drizzle with lemon juice.

2 To make the hemp-butter sauce, simmer the wine and shallots until they attain a marmalade consistency. Remove from the heat and blend with the chilled butter.

3 Add the hemp meal and hemp oil and salt and pepper to taste.

4 Place the fillets onto heated plates, surround with the sauce, and serve with rice.

tip: This fine and very delicate combination can also be made with other types of fish, such as trout or pike. Frying the pike perch in its skin locks in the juices and flavors.

ingredients

Salt
Pepper
8 pike perch fillets, about
  2 pounds total
Flour to coat fish
2 tablespoons clarified
  butter
Juice of $\frac{1}{2}$ lemon

hemp-butter sauce

1 cup white wine (light and
  dry, such as a blanc de
  blancs)
1 tablespoon finely diced
  shallots
10 tablespoons butter,
  chilled
$\frac{1}{3}$ cup hemp meal
2 tablespoons hemp oil
Salt
Pepper
2 cups basmati rice, cooked

hemp
81

honey-crusted duck breast
with hemp-seed sauce

ingredients

4 duck breasts, about
   9 ounces each
Salt
Pepper
1 tablespoon clarified
   butter
4 tablespoons honey
3 tablespoons port
3 tablespoons red wine
1 cup Meat Stock (page
   113) or bouillon
4 tablespoons roasted
   hemp seeds
3½ tablespoons butter,
   chilled

1 Wash the duck breasts in cold water and pat dry. Season with salt and pepper.

2 Melt clarified butter in a pan and fry the breasts, skin sides down, until crispy (about 10 minutes).

3 Remove from the pan and place onto a plate, skin sides up. Brush with honey and set aside in a warm place for at least 10 minutes.

4 Add port and red wine to the pan drippings and quickly reduce the sauce. Add Meat Stock and reduce again. Stir in hemp seeds and chilled butter. Remove from heat; the melting butter will thicken the sauce.

5 Cut the duck breasts into thin slices and arrange on plates with the sauce. Serve with parsnips and mashed potatoes.

hemp

hemp-stuffed chicken breast
with curry sauce and raisin rice

1 Slice the chicken breasts horizontally (like a sandwich), so that they can be opened.

2 Combine mustard, hemp meal, and herbs and smear onto the opened chicken breasts. Season with salt and pepper to taste.

3 Instead of closing the chicken breasts, roll them up. Using a piece of string, tie each roll as if it were a package and fry in butter over moderate heat for about 10 minutes, or until juicy. Remove from the pan and set aside in a warm place.

4 To make the sauce, sprinkle curry powder onto the pan drippings, add onion, and sauté briefly. Add Meat Stock and cream and thicken until creamy. Season with salt and pepper to taste.

5 Pour the rice into boiling water, reduce heat, and simmer for 15 to 20 minutes.

6 Meanwhile, soak the raisins for 15 to 20 minutes, drain in a strainer, and mix into the rice.

7 Slice the chicken breast into a fan shape, cover with the curry sauce, and serve with raisin rice.

ingredients

4 boneless chicken breasts,
  7 ounces each
1 1/2 tablespoons spicy
  mustard
1/3 cup hemp meal
Fresh herbs (thyme, parsley,
  tarragon, chervil), chopped
Salt
Pepper
Butter for frying

sauce
1 tablespoon curry powder
2 tablespoons finely diced
  onion
1/2 cup Meat Stock
  (page 113)
1/2 cup whipping cream
Salt
Pepper

rice
2 cups long-grain rice
  (such as basmati)
2/3 cup raisins

hemp
85

lamb chops
in hemp broth with green beans

ingredients

1 saddle of lamb
  (3½–4 pounds)
Salt

broth
5 tablespoons hemp seeds
2 onions
2 carrots
3 tablespoons celery root
2 cloves garlic
1 sprig of thyme
1 sprig of rosemary
Pinch of summer savory
2 quarts water
Pinch of salt

1 pound green beans,
  trimmed and washed
8 medium-sized potatoes,
  peeled and quartered

White pepper, freshly
  ground
4 tablespoons roasted
  hemp seeds
Hemp oil

1 Cut up the saddle of lamb into small chops, reserving the bones (or have your butcher prepare the meat for you). Lightly salt the chops.

2 To make the broth, brown the bones. Add hemp seeds, vegetables, herbs, and water. Simmer for about 3 hours.

3 Pass the broth through a strainer. Add salt and then boil the potatoes and green beans in the broth.

4 After 10 minutes, add the lamb chops and simmer the entire mixture at just above the boiling point for about 10 more minutes, or until lamb chops are rare, but not too rare.

5 Arrange broth, potatoes, beans, and lamb in deep bowls and sprinkle with pepper and hemp seeds. Garnish with a few drops of hemp oil.

pork rib roast
in hemp-beer sauce

1 Preheat oven to 350°.

2 Peel, core, and quarter the apples. Soak the prunes and raisins in apple juice for about 15 minutes.

3 Season the rib roast with salt and pepper, inside and out.

4 Mix the apples, prunes, and raisins with the bread crumbs and stuff into the rib cavity.

5 Close the opening with string and place in a roasting pan. Add about 2 cups water and place in preheated oven. Cook for about 2 hours. Baste the roast several times while it is cooking. Pour the hemp beer over the roast shortly before the end of the roasting period.

6 Remove the rib roast from the roasting pan. Pour the pan juices through a strainer into a pot, thicken with the beurre manié, and season to taste with salt and pepper.

7 Carve the roast into individual rib segments, arrange on heated plates, and serve with the hemp-beer sauce and potatoes.

serves eight

note: If hemp beer is not available (see "Hemp Resources, page 140), substitute a lager or a hefeweizen.

ingredients

5 apples (Gravenstein or Elstar)
5 ounces prunes
7 ounces raisins
1 cup apple juice
5½ pounds pork rib roast (brisket with ribs) prepared for stuffing
Salt
Pepper
⅔ cup bread crumbs
1 bottle of hemp beer
beurre manié (made with 4 tablespoons flour and 3 tablespoons softened butter)

hemp
89

medallions of venison
with a hemp crust

ingredients

3½ tablespoons butter,
  softened
¼ cup bread crumbs
⅓ cup hemp meal
Salt
Nutmeg
4 pounds venison
Pepper
Clarified butter

sauce
About 3½ pounds venison
  bones, including any meat
  left after boiling
2 tablespoons clarified
  butter
⅔ pound vegetables
  (carrots, celery, onions,
  garlic), trimmed and diced
1 tablespoon tomato paste
½ cup red wine
6 cups cold water
2 bay leaves
Salt
2 teaspoons peppercorns

1 Using a wire whisk, whip softened butter until fluffy. Add the bread crumbs and hemp meal, and season with salt and nutmeg to taste. Refrigerate.

2 Bone the venison. Cut into 12 uniform medallions and flatten lightly; set aside.

3 To make the sauce, chop the bones into small pieces and brown in clarified butter over high heat. After about 10 minutes, add the diced vegetables and continue to cook.

4 After about 5 minutes, add the tomato paste and continue to cook. Add the red wine, cold water, and bay leaves. Simmer lightly for about 3 hours, skimming off foam periodically.

5 Strain through a fine sieve. Bring to a boil and thicken. Season with salt and peppercorns to taste.

6 Season the medallions with salt and pepper. Sauté in clarified butter over medium heat for 6 to 8 minutes until pink.

7 Preheat the broiler. Cut the crust mixture into slices as large as the medallions, cover the medallions with the crust, and broil until the crust browns. Serve with the red-wine sauce and hand-shaved hemp spätzle (see recipe on page 66).

wild boar fillet
in a hemp crust on red cabbage salad

1 Salt and pepper the cleaned and dressed wild boar fillet. Roll in hemp meal and sauté in 3 tablespoons of the butter over medium heat (6 to 8 minutes) until pink. Place onto a heated plate.

2 Sauté the cabbage and onion in the remaining butter.

3 Add vinegar and apple juice and cook for about 5 minutes. The cabbage should remain firm.

4 Season to taste with salt and pepper and arrange the cabbage on plates.

5 Arrange the wild boar fillet on top of the cabbage and garnish with a sautéed apple slice.

ingredients

1-pound wild boar fillet
²/₃ cup hemp meal
6 tablespoons clarified
   butter
Small head of red cabbage,
   thinly sliced
1 tablespoon finely diced
   onion
3 tablespoons red wine
   vinegar
¹/₂ cup apple juice

1 apple (Gravenstein or
   Elstar), sliced

hemp
93

desserts

Hemp-accented
delicacies–the
perfect ending
to a meal

figs in hemp-beer batter
with hemp-almond sauce

ingredients

batter

¾ cup flour

2 tablespoons hemp meal

½ cup hemp beer (or any
   dark beer if not available)

2 eggs

Pinch of salt

sauce

½ cup roasted almond
   slices

Hemp-honey Sauce
   (page 108)

4 fresh figs

Oil for deep-frying

1 Using an electric hand mixer, beat the flour, hemp meal, hemp beer, eggs, and salt into a thick batter. Let stand for about 15 minutes.

2 To make the sauce, add the roasted almond slices to the Hemp-honey Sauce.

3 Rub the figs with a moist cloth. Holding the figs by the stem, dip briefly into the hemp-beer batter and fry in ¼-inch-deep hot oil (about 350°) for about 2 minutes, or until golden brown.

4 Remove figs from the oil and drip dry on a cloth. Cut in half and serve with the hemp-almond sauce while hot.

hemp-buttermilk pancakes
with pear and blueberry compote

ingredients

batter
1 cup flour
$\frac{1}{3}$ cup hemp meal
$\frac{1}{3}$ cup cornstarch
1 cup buttermilk
$\frac{1}{2}$ cup heavy cream
3 eggs
2 tablespoons sugar
Pinch of salt

compotes
4 pears
1 cup white wine
Pinch of cinnamon
8 tablespoons sugar

$\frac{1}{2}$ pound blueberries
3 tablespoons red wine
2 tablespoons butter, chilled

Powdered sugar for
  dusting

1 Combine flour, hemp meal, cornstarch, and buttermilk and stir until smooth. Let stand for 1 hour.

2 Thoroughly beat the eggs, 2 tablespoons sugar, and salt and mix with the batter.

3 Meanwhile, peel, quarter, and core the pears. Steam with the white wine, cinnamon, and 4 tablespoons sugar until soft.

4 Cook the blueberries with the red wine and 4 tablespoons sugar. Fold in the chilled butter.

5 Form the hemp-buttermilk batter into small pancakes and cook on a griddle over low heat until golden brown on both sides. Arrange the pancakes with the pear and blueberry compotes on plates and sprinkle with powdered sugar.

hemp-brittle parfait
with tipsy pears

note: This recipe must be started the day before, but it's definitely worth it.

1 On the first day, caramelize ½ cup sugar in a pan until light brown, then add the hemp seeds. Spread the resulting hemp brittle on a buttered baking sheet. Allow to cool completely and harden. Then finely chop the brittle with a large knife.

2 Beat the eggs, the egg yolk, and ½ cup sugar with a wire whisk, preferably in a mixing bowl over steam or in a double boiler until the sugar dissolves and a creamy mixture results. Continue to beat without steam for about 5 minutes.

3 Whip the cream until stiff. Stir about ⅓ of the whipped cream with the hemp brittle into the egg mixture. Using a rubber spatula, loosely fold the remaining ⅔ of the whipped cream and the walnut liqueur into the egg mixture. Pour into buttered cups and freeze for about 12 hours.

4 The next day, combine the red wine with 1 cup sugar and the cinnamon stick and bring to a boil. Add the pears. Simmer until soft and then allow to cool in the red wine.

5 Invert the parfaits onto plates, garnish with pears, and pour a little red wine over each parfait.

serves eight

ingredients

Prepare a day in advance:

2 cups sugar

¾ cup roasted hemp seeds

2 eggs

6 egg yolks

3 cups whipping cream

4 tablespoons walnut
  liqueur

4 cups red wine

1 cinnamon stick

8 pears, peeled, halved,
  and cored

hemp
101

hemp pudding

ingredients

Butter

Sugar (to sprinkle into the
   molds)

1 vanilla bean (slit open
   lengthwise)

$\frac{1}{2}$ cup whipping cream

5 tablespoons butter

$\frac{1}{2}$ cup flour

$\frac{1}{3}$ cup hemp meal

5 egg whites

4 egg yolks

$\frac{1}{4}$ cup sugar

Powdered sugar for dusting

1 Butter eight cups or small pudding molds and sprinkle with sugar.

2 Combine the vanilla bean and whipping cream in a pan, and bring to a boil. Remove from heat and set aside.

3 Preheat oven to 325°.

4 Prepare a roux with butter and flour. Add vanilla cream and hemp meal to the roux. Stir two egg whites into the warm mixture. Add the egg yolks and stir until smooth again. Beat the remaining egg whites with sugar until stiff and loosely fold into the mixture.

5 Pour into the prepared cups and place into a water bath. Bake for about 25 minutes.

6 Remove, dust with powdered sugar, and serve immediately.

serves eight

tip: As variations, try serving with Hemp-honey Sauce (see recipe on page 108) or with a summery berry compote. Be sure to extract the pudding by inverting the cups.

hemp and cheese dumplings
on plum compote

ingredients

dumplings

3 slices of white bread

1 cup ricotta cheese

¾ cup semolina

½ cup whipping cream

2 eggs

2 tablespoons melted
   butter

4 tablespoons hemp meal

compote

1 pound plums

½ cup red wine

⅓ cup sugar

1 cinnamon stick

¾ cup bread crumbs

½ cup sugar

1 To make the dumplings, remove the crusts from the bread and cut into small cubes. Press the cheese through a cloth. Combine with the bread cubes and the remaining ingredients to make a dough. Allow to sit in a cool place for at least 4 hours.

2 To make the compote, halve and stone the plums. Combine in a pot with red wine, sugar, and the cinnamon stick, and simmer over low heat for about 10 minutes.

3 Preheat oven to 350°.

4 Shape the cheese dough into uniform dumplings and drop them into boiling water. When the dumplings rise to the surface, remove and drip dry on a cloth. While the dumplings are cooking, combine the bread crumbs with the sugar and roast in a pan for about 5 minutes, or until golden brown.

5 Roll the cooked, dry dumplings in the bread crumbs and sugar mixture and arrange in deep dishes with the plum compote. Serve warm.

hemp and chocolate dumplings
with mint sauce

1 To make the dumplings, combine milk, sugar, butter, and cocoa and bring to a boil. Add semolina and stir with a ladle until the mixture separates from the pot.

2 Remove from the stove and add the beaten egg and the hemp meal to the hot mixture. Allow to cool.

3 Form small, uniform dumplings and simmer in sugar water until the dumplings rise to the surface.

4 To make the sauce, cut some of the mint into narrow strips and mix well with the remaining sauce ingredients.

5 Arrange the warm dumplings with the sauce on plates and garnish with whole mint leaves.

ingredients

dumplings
1 cup milk
3 tablespoons sugar
4 tablespoons butter
3 tablespoons cocoa powder
⅔ cup semolina
1 egg, beaten
⅓ cup hemp meal
Sugar water (made with 1 cup sugar and 8 cups water)

sauce
Fresh mint
1 cup yogurt
1 tablespoon honey
Lemon juice

Mint leaves

hemp
107

raisin noodles
in hemp-honey sauce

ingredients

noodles

½ cup raisins

1 tablespoon rum

2 pounds potatoes,
   boiled in their skins and
   cooked a day in advance

3 tablespoons ricotta
   cheese

⅓ cup flour

2 eggs

Clarified butter

sauce

3 egg yolks

2½ tablespoons honey

1 vanilla bean (slit open
   lengthwise)

1 cup whole milk

3 tablespoons hemp meal

Fresh mint

note: The potatoes should be cooked a day ahead of time.

1 Soak the raisins for ½ hour in the rum and a small amount of water.

2 Peel the potatoes and force through a strainer. Combine with cheese, flour, and eggs to make a dough.

3 To make the sauce, beat the egg yolks and honey together in a bowl. In a small saucepan, combine the vanilla bean with the milk and bring to a boil. Pour over the egg yolk and honey mixture.

4 Sprinkle hemp meal on top and gently reheat the entire mixture until it becomes creamy. (Do not allow to boil.)

5 Add the soaked raisins to the potato dough; place the dough on a floured surface and shape into finger-thick noodles.

6 Fry the raisin noodles in clarified butter over moderate heat until golden brown.

7 Arrange raisin noodles and hemp-honey sauce on plates and serve with fresh mint.

zabaglione
with hemp, bananas, and chocolate ice cream

1 Place hemp meal, white wine, sugar, eggs, and egg liqueur into a double boiler. Beat well with a wire whisk until a foamy cream results.

2 Peel the bananas, cut into slices of any size, and distribute onto four ovenproof plates. Pour the cream over the bananas and broil until pale yellow.

3 Serve with chocolate ice cream and mint.

tip: Serve this dessert with a cup of espresso and you'll have the perfect ending to a delicious meal.

ingredients

4 tablespoons hemp meal
1 cup white wine
⅔ cup sugar
2 eggs
3 tablespoons egg liqueur
  (optional)

2 bananas

Chocolate ice cream
Fresh mint

hemp
111

basic recipes

fish stock

about 4¼ cups
Bones and skin of 2 fish and
2 fish heads
1 onion, finely diced
1 clove garlic
2 stalks celery, diced
1 small leek, diced
1 carrot, diced
1 tablespoon olive oil
1 bay leaf
1 sprig of thyme
1 tomato
½ cup white wine

1 Remove the fins and gills from the fish and dis-
card. Carefully rinse the bones and heads in cold
water and remove all traces of blood.

2 Braise the onion, garlic, and vegetables in olive
oil for about 1 minute.

3 Add the bones, heads, spices, and the tomato.
Add white wine and 3½ cups cold water. Bring
the entire mixture to a boil and skim off the
resulting foam. Boil lightly for about 15 minutes
and then simmer for another 15 minutes.

4 Carefully pass the stock through a fine strainer.

meat stock

1 Rinse the beef brisket with cold water. Bring to a boil in 4 quarts of water. Skim off the foam.

2 Add the vegetables, bay leaves, allspice, and clove, and boil for 1½ hours.

3 Strain through a fine sieve and season to taste with salt, pepper, and nutmeg.

tip: The beef brisket that was cooked to make the Meat Stock can be served with horse-radish sauce and boiled potatoes as a main course.

ingredients

12 cups
2 pounds beef brisket
1 bunch of vegetables (1 carrot, ½ leek, 1 celery stalk, 1 onion), chopped
2 bay leaves
1 teaspoon allspice berries
1 clove
Salt
Pepper
Nutmeg

vegetable stock

1 Wash the vegetables and cut into cubes. Braise lightly in butter and add the cold water. Bring to a boil and skim off the foam. Add the bay leaf and herbs and simmer lightly for about 1 hour.

2 Pass through a fine strainer.

tip: Stocks can be frozen in ice cube trays. The cubes can then be used in individual portions.

8 cups
1⅓ cups carrots, cubed
⅔ cup leeks, cubed
1 fennel root
1 onion
2 stalks of celery
2 tomatoes
2 tablespoons clarified butter
10 cups cold water
1 bay leaf
Herbs to taste

the hemp idea

Recently, hemp has become synonymous with renewable resources.

Because of the battle that has been waged in the media and in the courts against the prohibition of the cultivation of hemp, this plant has risen to a summit of attention that flax and Chinese reed never attained. The sheer variety of potential hemp-derivative product lines is fascinating even to a conventional business, while the plant's medicinal and psychotropic aspects surround it with an aura of mystery.

Today, the world is in the middle of serious restructuring. Finite natural resources are being exhausted; we must phase the end of mass production into our industrial paradigm and at the same time deal with the globalization of information, goods, and services. While hemp by itself is unable to solve all problems of a modern society, it can become a model for new paths to growth and employment with regional economies.

The important products at issue are: insulation materials for residential construction and vehicle manufacturing, raw cellulose for the paper industry, textile fibers, oil, and energy. These products may, for example, replace fiberglass and mineral fiber, both products whose manufacture requires tremendous amounts of fossil fuel (and the corresponding high emissions of CO_2). The raw materials supplied by hemp are generated by photosynthesis, i.e., primarily as a result of solar energy. In this process, they absorb the CO_2 that

threatens our climate from the surrounding air. Advances in information technology now make it possible to interconnect regional cycles, so that regionally produced but uniformly defined and designed products can be distributed in large markets.

Where do we stand today? The agricultural problems of hemp cultivation (such as seed-harvesting technology) have been largely resolved. Initial processing of the plant, i.e., the separation of the fibers from the wooden portion of the plant (the shives), did present a bottleneck. Existing technology was designed entirely for processing previous product lines, particularly textile fibers.

the hemp idea

For various reasons, however, these types of
textile fibers are not well suited for introducing a
new raw material into the market. However, the
expensive textile technology resulted in excessive
prices for simple insulation materials. Therefore, a
new, inexpensive, and mobile extraction technology was developed that can be applied using circles
of machinery.

**New economic cycles
also require new
industrial planning.**

The hemp factory in Zehdenick, north of
Berlin, utilizes existing industrial buildings (a for-
mer cable plant). The mineral fiber industry
purchased the used central machine line (matted
fiber equipment with needling equipment) and
reconfigured it for processing hemp. The project
was only made possible by the fact that the inve-
stors were not dependent on bank loans
and subsidized funds (used machinery is not
subsidized and bank loans are not provided for
leased property).

hemp
118

**In addition to the regional
value creation cycles,
existing major industrial
customers must be
supplied with natural fibers.**

Another hemp factory began production in 1998
in Lutomia, Poland, and another, an official Expo
2000 project, is
currently under
construction
in Dessau,

Germany. Negotiations for an addi-tional project are under way with the city of Wolfs-burg, Germany, in addition to two large hemp factories near Arad, Romania. Regardless of one's opinion of the auto-mobile, it would certainly represent an enormous step in the direction of permanen-cy and an economy based on recycling if seat covers, floor coverings, upholstery, and fiber compound materials were to be made of natural fibers instead of synthetic materials. To achieve this objective, however, it must be convin-cingly demonstrated that the significant demand for these materials can be met. An individual region cannot do this. This can only be achieved by a group of associated regions.

Because biomass is the workhorse of the decen-tralized energy supply of the future, we will deve-lop biogas reactors for hemp. We hope that we will also be able to extract a fiber from these reactors that will be especially well suited for cellulose production. Further developments in repulping technology will lead to finer textile

We need a readily applica-ble supplement to wind and solar energy, which are not always available.

fibers. In the meantime, using existing technology, a complete kit for single-family home construction, based on local materials such as wood, clay, and hemp, has already been developed.

We must try new creative ways to reach those who have not yet been convinced that a sus-

tainable economy is a necessary key to a secure future. Hemp recipes may be part of that creative key. This would not be the first revolution that began In the kitchen. Furthermore, as along as we claim to be improving the world, we should avoid the common mistake of boring those we're trying to convince. Hemp dishes provide exciting and entertaining ways of taking advantage of human curiosity about alternative food products to stimulate interest in the facts behind such products.

the history of hemp

10,000 B.C.	Hemp is cultivated in China to manufacture textiles, as a food product, and as a medicine
5500 B.C.	Earliest archaeological evidence of cannabis seeds in the area that is currently Germany (Eisenberg, Thuringia)
3700 B.C.	First written mention of hemp in the *Pen Tsao*, a Chinese medical book written by the Emperor Chen Nung
484 B.C.	Herodotus reports on the use of hemp among the Scythians and the Thracians
800 A.D.	Charles the Great proclaims a law mandating that hemp must be cultivated in his empire
1150	In her medical works, Hildegard von Bingen studies the medicinal properties of hemp, among those of other plants
1455	The *Gutenberg Bible,* printed on hemp paper, is completed
~1500	Until the 20th century, hemp is mentioned in virtually every medical book
1765	George Washington, the first president of the United States, plants hemp
1912	Hemp is included in the list of prohibited substances at the International Opium Conference.
1924	The 2nd International Opium Conference proclaims a worldwide drug control law and places hemp on the list of prohibited substances
~1939	Hemp cultivation becomes necessary worldwide (due to the war and the resulting disruption of import routes for fiber plants)
1945	After the war, hemp cultivation in the Western world decreases to a virtually insignificant level
1960s	Millions of Americans use marijuana recreationally
1980	First International Cannabis Conference in Amsterdam
1996	The cultivation of low-THC hemp is once again permitted in Germany
1998	Non-THC hemp production begins in Canada

Sources: Hemp Museum, Berlin, and "The History of Hemp" from the Arkansas Law Reform Group.

the revolution
in the kitchen

Everything started with a hemp dinner that demonstrated how hemp products can enrich the kitchen.

Everyone should be talking about hemp. Ralf Hiener proved why this is so with his hemp dinner, which he conjured up in January 1998 for eighty guests in Berlin's HanfContor The guests are still raving about the dinner today. This encouraged us to institutionalize hemp cuisine.

The following outlets in Germany promote hemp dishes:

• A snack bar, the Hemp Kitchen, at Senefelder Platz in the Prenzlauer Berg district. Here, new snacks and dishes made with hemp are constantly being presented and the public's reaction tested.
• A restaurant, the French Quarter. Just a few steps away from the snack bar, at the Schwedter corner of Choriner Strasse, hemp-accented Cajun dishes and a rotating assortment of hemp specialties are presented in an atmosphere reminiscent of the American South.
• The HanfContor next to the snack bar, is an attractive dining hall. This is where the hemp dinner, the tradition initiated by Ralf Hiener, is continued every Wednesday evening. Here, chefs are given the opportunity to let their imaginations run wild when it comes to hemp.

In addition to the above, guests are given the opportunity to get to know other industrial products created from hemp. Fashion shows, stock market evenings, jazz brunches, and just plain good music all contribute to educating through entertainment. These efforts can be replicated throughout the world.

Sponsored trips can also encourage interest: participation in the harvest on German, Polish, Hungarian, or Romanian farms; visits to the glass house museum village, where the traditional hemp economy is demonstrated; tours of the hemp factories in Zehdenick, Dessau, Lutomia (in Poland), and Arad (in Romania). There, courses in spinning, weaving, manufacturing felt and floor coverings, cooking, baking, and paper manufacturing all demonstrate the versatility of hemp.

We are convinced that many people will prefer to spend their leisure time engaged in practical activities and learning instead of simply passing the time as consumers. And many of them will no longer be able to forget the issue of hemp as a driving force for new economic cycles. In this manner, the revolution will come from the kitchen.

the hemp entrepreneur

I come from a village in Germany, so I missed the hippie era. Later, I went on to study law and knew nothing about hemp until 1991. My route to this renewable raw material passed through the classic environmental protection movement.

We believed in warning and giving notice, flyers inciting readers to action, and long meetings in political groups. However, the protective and instructional aspect of environmental protection was not satisfying for me. What could we do to secure lasting social and economic structures? In any event, it makes sense to replace destructive materials and energy cycles with those that can be operated over the long term, while at the same time preserving our country and our countryside.

In 1991, a professor at Humboldt University introduced me to hemp, its history, and its advantages. In 1993, I founded the Hemp Society, together with Matthias Bröcker (the author of the *Hemp Bible*), agricultural societies, and agricultural scientists. We went to court to sue for the legalization of hemp cultivation, which had been prohibited in Germany until then.

In 1995 I was forced to decide whether to continue as a judge with a secure government job or to take the plunge. I opted to give up my secure existence and my pension claim to become a hemp entrepreneur. All I can say to you today is this: no risk, no fun. It is a great feeling to have placed my bets on the right horse and to watch as risk is slowly transformed into security.

Matthias Schillo, born in 1949 in Oberlöstern in the Saarland, is the executive director of TreuHanf AG and the managing director of TreuHanf Investment GmbH & Co. KG in Brandenburg and Saxony-Anhalt

hemp
125

the chef

As a chef, I am always interested in discovering new ingredients. But for me, this doesn't mean joining in the race to find the latest exotic novelty designed to produce a quick impact. Instead, I have my sights set on regional cuisine. I much prefer a food product that can be bought fresh in a market over some extravagant frozen culinary item wrapped in plastic that's traveled a long way to get to me. In this regard, hemp is certainly our most recent discovery. Of course, we don't have to make this into some philosophical movement right off the bat. After all, I've eaten hemp burgers or hemp cakes that tasted so bland they were nothing but poor advertisements for hemp. However, when used sparingly, carefully, in the right place, and at the right time, hemp can be right on the mark and complete a dish. It can add the finishing touch to a creation and introduce our taste buds to a brand new world. It's not only taste, but also consistency, crunchiness, and the sometimes nutty-pungent aroma with which hemp elevates many a dish from the usual assortment. Hemp is not the easiest and most inexpensive ingredient to use. But once you become involved with hemp and figure out its complexities, your efforts will be rewarded many times over. Let's see if hemp can take over the kitchen once more. It promises to be an exciting adventure.

Ralf Hiener,
a fourth-generation chef
born in South Baden in
1966, has been living in
West Pomerania since 1994

the restaurateur

I became aware of hemp as a raw material when I read Jack Herer's book, *The Emperor Wears No Clothes: Hemp and the Marijuana Conspiracy*. That was in 1993. Naturally, I had known of hemp as a narcotic for some time, but under a different name. But now I was unable to let go of the idea of hemp as a crop, and it began to find its way into my daily life and into our restaurant: as the paper on which menus are printed, as material for uniforms, as soap and detergent for daily use, and, of course, in the form of seeds and oil used in the kitchen. The fact that hemp was able to achieve this status in our restaurant was certainly not accidental, because we valued doing business in an environmentally sensitive manner, even in our small business.

Our lifestyle toward the end of the twentieth century has become so destructive and so imbued with hopelessness that I am convinced we cannot continue along this path. That's just one of the reasons I support hemp. To the best of my knowledge, the use of hemp makes sense ecologically, as well as from a long-term economic perspective. We do not have that many alternatives at our disposal that we can afford to simply ignore one alternative or another. I look forward to hemp making its comeback!

Bettina Mack, born in the Upper Palatinate region in 1963, has been an independent gastronome in the town of auf dem Darsse since 1994

the writer

In Berlin, it is virtually impossible to ignore the hemp movement. There are conferences on the subject of hemp, hemp parades, magazines sold at kiosks, and hemp shops, and you can drink hemp beer in quite a few bars. In fact, it seems fair to say that hemp is already making its way into our daily culture. When I heard that Bettina and Ralf had started cooking with hemp, I was confronted with a completely new aspect of this material. I was completely surprised by the first hemp dish I tasted. There was nothing ascetic or biodynamically theoretical about it. Instead of tasting like "rabbit food" it tasted exciting and interesting. Let's hope that the current commotion around hemp is not just a fad that will soon pass. I believe that a little faith in hemp is certainly called for. It has too many arguments in its favor. And that's not the half of it. After all, hemp enjoys a certain "flair." Hated and prohibited by some, loved and worshiped by others, it will certainly find its rightful place. In any case, I wish hemp all the best and plenty of staying power in making its comeback, even in the kitchen.

Stefan Wirner, born in the Upper Palatinate region in 1966, has been living in Berlin as a freelance writer since 1990

epilogue

Why do we keep devising new limits for toxic substances in the ground and atmosphere? Let us accept what nature has given us and take advantage of the abundant possibilities offered by hemp.

No other useful plant can be cultivated in such an environmentally friendly manner—with little fertilizer and no pesticides whatsoever—while providing such an abundant and varied harvest.

Hemp cultivation was prohibited for decades in many countries. The history of this prohibition reads like a crime thriller. After hemp had been demonized as "marijuana—the devil's drug of our youth," the hemp prohibition took hold in the United States before World War II and, from there, spread to virtually the entire world. Nonetheless, both the Americans ("hemp for victory") and the Nazis forced its cultivation during the war. It is interesting to note that the term "hemp" was always used when this plant was needed, but that it was referred to as "marijuana" when the intention was to discourage its use.

Now, at the end of the century, we still do not know how to approach hemp in a normal, uninhibited way. Supporters of hemp have already presented many

arguments in its favor: Not a single tree has to be cut down to make hemp paper, which also happens to be a durable and high-quality material. Clothing made of hemp is more durable and its production considerably more environmentally compatible than clothing made of cotton, particularly as cotton cultivation requires the use of substantial amounts of pesticides and water. Are these truly just flimsy arguments brought forward by people whose only interest is to pave the way for the legalization of a drug? Certainly not.

The overall outlook is certainly not discouraging. According to the lyrics of a song by Bob Marley, "you can fool some people some time, but you can't fool all the people all the time." And in fact, the time when the hashish phobia could be used to strangle any discussion about hemp as a useful crop seems to have passed. The resulting hemp movement could certainly be successful. Perhaps this cookbook can make a contribution in this direction. We certainly hope so.

Naturally, one cannot expect too much of hemp. And some of what has been written about the issue does seem a little exaggerated. Hemp will not save the world and will not eliminate world

By now, people are beginning to realize that the hemp prohibition created more harm than good.

hunger. Ultimately, anything that banks on or promises absolute and total solutions should be approached with care. However, it ought to be possible—especially in light of the world's immense environmental problems—to give hemp a new chance as a useful plant. In a progressive society, it ultimately makes more sense to utilize the advantages of a valuable renewable resource than to completely ignore this plant, simply in the interest of punishing marijuana smokers.

Flexibility and modernization: catchwords of our time. Adjusting to new circumstances and responding to them in an appropriate manner—an option that hemp gives us.

It is precisely hemp, a plant that is highly durable and grows under a wide variety of climatic conditions, that could become the symbol of a new flexibility, a flexibility that allows us to play a less destructive role in the cycle of nature. In this light, modernization can also mean remembering and reviving a good thing.

This opinion has long been held by everyone who contributed to the development of this cookbook. It is certainly about time to reawaken our curiosity about the possibilities of this ancient, virtually forgotten "herb". The future is always full of possibility. Let us play a role in shaping that future by cultivating, harvesting, using, enjoying, and eating hemp!

glossary

Grass: Dried leaves (and flowers) of the cannabis plant that are smoked because of their narcotic effects; often referred to as "weed."

Hashish, marijuana: A narcotic extracted from the resin of Indian hemp.

Hemp: (cannabis sativa), a genus of the mulberry plant (as is its closest relative, hops). Hemp is an annual plant with greenish leaves and nutlike fruits (seeds).

One differentiates among the following varieties: *cannabis sativa* (thick, fibrous stalks up to 13 feet in height, low-to no-THC content), *cannabis indica* (up to 4 feet in height, high-THC content), and *cannabis ruderalis* (2 feet in height, relatively non-fibrous stalks, varying-THC content).

Hemp fiber: As one of the bast fibers, hemp fiber is one of the most valuable and fertile plant fibers of all. For many centuries, hemp played an important role in the manufacture of sailcloth,

ropes, cables, etc., and was valued for its substanti-al resistance to moisture. The hemp fiber supplies a high-quality cellulose that is well suited for the production of paper. The oldest paper in the world, made in China, was made of hemp fibers, as was the *Gutenberg Bible*.

Hemp meal: ground hemp seeds

Hemp seeds: nutlike, green to gray fruits of the cannabis plant

Hemp straw: a harvest product of hemp, it is separated into fibers and shives

Hemp shives: the small interior of the stem of the cannabis plant which has been broken into pieces

THC: Tetrahydrocannabinol; substance in the cannabis plant to which the narcotic effect is ascribed; also a therapeutic agent that can be used to treat a wide variety of diseases.

hemp
137

legal status

Cultivation of hemp, regardless of variety remains illegal in the United States. Several states including Montana, Virginia, New Hampshire, North Dakota, Tennessee, New Mexico, and Minnesota (through legislation backed by Gov. Jesse Ventura) have moved toward making it legal. Hawaii has agreed to a 10-acre test crop. But while there is interest at the state level, these efforts will not amount to much until the federal government relents.

Proponents of banning cultivation claim that while there are low-TCH varieties, these can be used to camouflage the growth of high-THC varieties, since drug enforcement agents rely on aerial searches to detect marijuana fields. Both the Drug Enforcement Agency and the White House's Office of National Drug Control Policy support continuing the ban on hemp production, claiming that it would send the wrong message to young people. Pro-hemp forces say trying to grow THC-laden marijuana in low-THC hemp plants would dilute the marijuana plants, hurting the potency of the illegal, high-cash crop. Police counter that this would work in reverse as well, producing a hemp with THC content.

Throughout the world, in more than 20 countries, hemp has been cultivated for a

variety of products including cosmetics, beer, plastics, and paper. Canada began hemp production in 1998 and 6,000 acres were planted, yielding profits up to $200 an acre during a period when farmers of traditional crops such as wheat were struggling just to break even. A 1998 University of Kentucky study estimated hemp could bring farmers up to $600 an acre. A North Dakota State University research study indicated that hemp is a useful rotation crop for wheat and potato farmers.

Hemp and Health

A few words on the digestibility of food products made of hemp: Some have warned against the use of hemp in food products. The claim was that small trace amounts of THC in food products made of hemp could have adverse effects on the health of consumers. Others respond to this claim as follows: "Hemp seeds and hemp oil themselves contain no drug substances, particularly not the primary drug known as tetrahydrocannabinol (THC). . . . Small amounts of THC can only find their way into food products as a result of insufficient removal of the surrounding leaves and inadequate cleaning of the seeds. . . . The many tests that have been conducted . . . have shown that the majority of hemp-based food products contain insignificantly small residual amounts of THC, amounts which preclude any physical or psychological effects."*

* From *Hemp, The Cannabis Magazine*, 12/1997.

hemp
139

hemp resources

Because the commercial use of hemp is expanding so rapidly, the following should only be considered a sampling of available resources. At the very least be sure to check out the hemp search engines on the world wide web listed below.

Hemp Search Engines

(searchable by region and product)
www.hempseed.com
www.hemptech.com

See also:

Ohio Hempery
(www.hempery.com). This web site archives almost 1000 articles related to hemp.

Publications

Books

Bócsa, Iván. *The Cultivation of Hemp: Botany, Varieties, Cultivation, and Harvesting*, Sebastopal, CA: Hemptech, 1998.

Conrad, Chris. *Hemp for Health: the Medicinal and Nutritional Uses of Cannabis Sativa,*

Conrad, Chris. *Hemp: Lifeline to the Future: The Unexpected Answer for Our Environmental and Economic Recovery*, Los Angeles: Creative Xpressions Publications, 1994.

Herer, Jack. *Hemp and the Marijuana Conspiracy: The Emperor Wears No Clothes*, 11th ed., Van Nuys, CA: HEMP Publications, 1998. *This is the book that inspired many of the people involved in the making of* The Hemp Cookbook. *Check out the author's web site at www.jackherer.com.*

Kane, Mari. *Hemp Pages: The Hemp Industry Source Book 1999–2000*, Forestville, CA: HempWorld, 1999. www.hempworld.com.

Leson, Gero, et al. *Hemp Foods and Oils for Health*, Bookmasters (800) 265-4367 or Ohio Hempery (800) buy-hemp.

Ranalli, Paolo, ed. *Advances in Hemp Research*, Binghamton, NY: The Haworth Press, Inc. (Food Products Press) www.haworthpressinc.com.

Robinson, Rowan. *The Hemp Manifesto: 101 Ways That Hemp Can Save Our World.*

Robinson, Rowan and Nelson, Robert A. *The Great Book of Hemp: The Complete Guide to the Commercial and Medicinal Uses of the World's Most Extraordinary Plant*, Rochester, VT: Park Street Press, 1996.

Roulac, John W. *Hemp Horizons: The Comeback of the World's Most Promising Plant*, White River Junction, VT: Chelsea Green Publications, 1997.

Magazines

HempWorld Magazine
HempWorld
PO Box 550
Forestville, CA 95436
(800) 659-4421
http://www.hempworld.com

Hemp Times
New York, NY
retail store: Planet Hemp

For current hemp legislation:

www.hempseed.com/hempseed/
bills99.html

Eric Steenstra
Ecolution/CyberHemp
PO Box 2279
Merrifield, VA 22116
(703) 207-9001
http://www.ecolution.com

North American Industrial
Hemp Council
PO Box 259329
Madison, WI 53725-9329
(608) 258-0243
www.naihc.org

Agro-Tech Communications
7344 Raleigh Lagrange Rd.
Cordova, TN 38018
Ph: (901) 757-1777
Fax: (901) 937-7884
www.agrotechfiber.com

Johnny Appleseed, Inc.
55 Broad Street, 23rd floor
New York, NY 10004
Ph: (212) 344-5907
Fax: (212) 344-0974
e-mail: www.hempseed.com

Events
Santa Cruz Industrial Hemp Expo
(831) 425-3003

Food

Rella Foods
PO Box 5020
Santa Rosa, CA 95402
(707) 571-1330
www.rella.com
For an excellent source of information
on hemp as food (how
to prepare it, clean it, etc.) try
www.rella.com/hempfood.html

Boulder Hemp Company
Heavenly Hemp Foods
PO Box 1794
Nederland, CO 80466
(888) eat-hemp
www.hempfoods.com

Mama Indica's Hemp Seed Treats
(250) 725-4288
www.isalnd.net/~mama

Zima Foods
Victoria BC, Canada
Hemp food company

Willie's Hemp Soda
San Rafael, CA

True Nature Foods,
Boulder Creek, CA
Pre-made hemp foods

Beer

Henflings
Ben Lomond CA
Hemp beer and wine

Frederick Brewing Company
4607 Wedgwood Boulevard
Frederick, MD 21703
(888) 258-7434
www.hempanale.com

Kentucky Hemp Beer Company
401 Cross Street
Lexington, KYU 40508
(606) 252-6004
www.hempbeerco.com

Seeds

Boulder Hemp Company
Heavenly Hemp Foods
PO box 1794
Nederland, CO 80466
(888) eat-hemp
www.hempfoods.com

Ohio Hempery, Inc.
www.hempery.com

The Hemp Corporation
PO Box 1368
Santa Rosa, CA95402
(707) 527-5711

recipes
from a to z

74 **Bouillabaisse** of Freshwater Fish with Hemp and Dumplings

26 **Carpaccio of Beef** with Hemp Oil and Romano

33 **Cucumber Soup** with Hemp Dumplings

96 **Figs in Hemp-beer Batter** with Hemp-almond Sauce

78 **Fillet of Pike** with Hemp-horseradish Crust

112 **Fish Stock**

58 **Hemp and Cabbage Strudel**

104 **Hemp and Cheese Dumplings** on Plum Compote

107 **Hemp and Chocolate Dumplings** with Mint Sauce

54 **Hemp and Potato Gratin**

56 **Hemp and Potato Dumplings** with Tomato-leek Garnish

62 **Hemp and Saffron Risotto** with Chanterelles

65 **Hemp and Sage Polenta** with Pan-roasted Bell Peppers

49 **Hemp-and-Vegetable Ravioli** on Red Lentils

101 **Hemp-brittle Parfait** with Tipsy Pears

98 **Hemp-buttermilk Pancakes** with Pear-elderberry Compote

61 **Hemp Crepes** with Mushrooms

50 **Hemp Gnocchi** with Curried Carrots

34 **Hemp-pancake Soup**

46 **Hemp Patties**

102 **Hemp Pudding**

38 **Hemp Quiche**

53 **Hemp-semolina Slices** with Chanterelle Mushrooms

18 **Hemp Snack**

66 **Hemp Spätzle** with Tomatoes and Goat Cheese

77 **Hemp-steamed Cod** with Dill Sauce

85 **Hemp-stuffed Chicken Breast** with Curry Sauce and Raisin Rice

41 **Hemp-tomato Crostini**

37 **Hemp-vegetable Soup**

82 **Honey-crusted Duck Breast** with Hemp-seed Sauce

86 **Lamb Chops** in Hemp Broth with Green Beans

29 **Lamb's Lettuce** with Hemp-potato Vinaigrette

113 **Meat Stock**

90 **Medallions of Venison** with a Hemp Crust

30 **Mixed Greens** with Hemp Oil and Hemp Seeds

81 **Pike-perch Fillet** with Hemp-butter Sauce

89 **Pork Rib Roast** in Hemp-beer Sauce

69 **Potato Dumplings** with a Hemp Filling

42 **Potato Salad** with Hemp-oil Vinaigrette

108 **Raisin Noodles** in Hemp-honey Sauce

70 **Spaghetti** with Hemp and Almond Pesto

113 **Vegetable Stock**

93 **Wild Boar Fillet** in a Hemp Crust on Red Cabbage Salad

111 **Zabaglione** with Hemp, Bananas, and Chocolate Ice Cream

Ten Speed Press
P.O. Box 7123
Berkeley, California 94707
www.tenspeed.com

Distributed in Canada by Ten Speed Press Canada, in New
Zealand by Southern Publishers Group, in Australia by Simon
and Schuster Australia, in South Africa by Real Books, in
Singapore and Malaysia by Berkeley Books, and in the United
Kingdom and Europe by Airlift Books.

Translation assistance by Advanced Linguistic Services, Berkeley,
California.

Library of Congress Cataloging-in-Publication Data
Hiener, Ralf, 1966–
    [Kochbuch. English]
    The hemp cookbook / Ralf Hiener; Bettina Mack;
photography Ansgar Pudenz
        p.   cm.
    Includes bibliographical references (p.   ).
    ISBN 1-58008-105-3
    1. Cookery (Hemp)   I. Mack, Bettina, 1963– .   II. Title
TX814.5.H45H53 1999
    641.6'353--dc21   99-26952
                                                        CIP

First Printing, 1999
Printed in Germany

1 2 3 4 5 6 7 8 9 10 – 03 02 01 00 99